INLAY WITH NACRE

The Names of Forgotten Women

CINDY WILLIAMS GUTIÉRREZ

Willow Books

Detroit, Michigan

Inlay with Nacre: The Names of Forgotten Women

Copyright © 2019 by Cindy Williams Gutiérrez

Editor: Randall Horton

Cover art: © Cristina Acosta

ISBN 978-1-7322091-1-4

LCCN 2019934835

Willow Books, a Division of Aquarius Press

www.WillowLit.net

Printed in the United States of America

In memory of my mother

Her face has disappeared. This happens
more often than you think…

—Andrea Hollander

Contents

Acknowledgments   7

For Remembering   9

I   **11**

Arranged Marriage   13

When I Look   14

Columbia Gorge Dance Card   15

What She Said When I Smiled at Her across the Table   16

Dear Impostor,   18

Warranty   19

Hair   20

C-Word   21

Tourist-attraction.com   22

My body   23

Congolese Calculus   24

Confession   29

Enheduanna's Curse on Lugalanne   31

#TippiHedrenToo   32

In Brazil's Defense   33

Widow's Choice   35

Proverbs for Pashtun Women   36

Postcards from Croatia   37

Legend of the Young Storyteller   38

A Note Sor Juana Dreams of Sending to the Bishop of Puebla   39

II	**41**
To My Mother	43
An Embarrassment of Euphemisms	44
Eugenics Rant	45
Kali Knocks on a Mother's Door	47
A Mother's Answer to Slavery in Toni Morrison's Beloved Story	48
I Did Not Name You El Negro	49
Your face	51
A Linguist Stick Speaks Up	52
Blackbird's Revenge	53
Editorial on the Trinity: Mother, Sister, Bishop	54
Mary Magdalene's Canticle	55
Ballad of the Crone	57
Fortune Teller	58
Message from the Black Madonna to the First Mothers	60
Hand	61
Song for Nacre	62
The Daughter I Sometimes Have	63
Letter from Camille Claudel to Albert Einstein	64
Dream Diary: Artist Sketch	66
In the Cypress and Cedar Box	68
Willow	69
Dream Diary: Invocation	70
Notes	72
Source Acknowledgments	78
About the Author	79

Acknowledgments

My love to Michael for our shared life in the Northwest hinterlands which has opened a space for creation. My gratitude to Literary Arts for a 2016 Oregon Literary Fellowship which encouraged the making of this manuscript. In admiration and appreciation of Nicholas D. Kristof and Sheryl WuDunn whose courageous advocacy of women initiated the impulse for this body of work. My thanks to Randall Horton for believing in this collection and to Aquarius Press for their commitment to underrepresented voices.

Heartfelt gratitude to Dr. Craig Santos Perez for his guidance in deepening these poems. With appreciation for the valuable critique of Joan Houlihan, Rusty Morrison, and my fellow poets in the Colrain Manuscript Conference which freed me to expand my vision. My muse thanks Daemond Arrindell for his illuminating workshop on ekphrastic poetry, Béalleka for her provocative seminar on Toni Morrison's *Beloved*, Albert Trople for his indignation over Sister McBride, and Russell J. Young and Jonathan Torgovnik for their luminous photographs of Croatia and the Congo, respectively.

Special thanks to Andrea Hollander for her edifying epigraph and to the rest of the Pearl Poets of Portland, Oregon for ten marvelous years of shared insight and friendship. My gratitude to the Confluence Poets of Twisp, Washington for our new-found camaraderie and imaginative germination of poems. *Mil gracias por el apoyo y el cariño de Los Porteños,* Portland's Latino writers' collective.

For Remembering

Begin with a box made of cypress and cedar:

A golden elephant finial. (Bodes good luck in the next life.)

Letters, postcards, and ransom notes. To personages real and imagined.

One coutil wedding corset and a collage of newspaper articles. (News flees while editorials leave a lasting impression. So does a corset.)

Untolled bells, uncast ballots and spells.

Raven quills, blackbird feathers. Tarot cards of rearing bears.

Dance cards and dream diaries. (Forget daily journals since heavenly Morpheus and the hearth-bound Pentates refuse to cohabitate.)

Crushed crayon books, charred poems, and words ripped from dictionaries.

Warranties (preferably lifetime).

Sepia photographs of the disappeared, and disappearing.

Prisms. And pressed white irises. (Though indigo will summon the Goddess and guide your dead.)

Hair (not locks: braids, tresses, manes of hair).

Close box. Inlay with nacre the names of forgotten women. Inhale the fragrance.

I

Arranged Marriage

Dutiful silence   cinches her torso
like a skeletal   coutil corset   this

carapace of bones.   lacing blushes
darker than   ardent

spirits   silk   threading eyelets
like blood-   shot streamers.

maidhood   stripped   two
ribbons crossed   with tautness

until   dizzy   she swoons
against the rock   in her chest.

When I Look

I see blazing trousseaus
surrounded by wan walls primed with gesso.
I see a cadmium-red bed with indigo pillow.
You see a nude on blankets of cobalt blue.
I say, *Paint me with your fingers where it will not show.*
You pose me with turpentine hands, send me reeling.
I see scarlet suitcases in a peeling-
dun corner of a gray railway depot.

I feel corrugated color:
the tug to move, to stray, to flee—
until a flaxen sun lightens the air.
Your face in dazzling relief:
I am ready to step down, step into, for—
I am ready to blur.

Columbia Gorge Dance Card

Even the noble pine cannot resist the wind's advances.
With uneven breath, he curls along her stoic spine,

refusing no for an answer. No question
he's notorious in dance circles on the Columbia.

Milonga campera—titillating tango:
Gorge wind leads, faithless fir cuts in—follows.

A sea of lithe, green lines.
Gusty tempo and her branches sway, sashay

until spiked cones slip off like lusty stilettos.
The ardor of the *bandoñeón* swells, bellows.

At the river's edge, I shift my listless weight
from foot to foot, surrender. Desire—brushfire,

volcano, when will you erupt this space
between us into grasses wild as pampas?

What She Said When I Smiled at Her across the Table

You have beautiful teeth.
Teeth matter:
bad ones create havoc in your body.
The dentist claims mine are trouble,
my sinuses too. Doctor says
he may need to operate if I don't feel better,

and I'd like to, but I don't bet
I will—with a deviated septum, mercury in my teeth.
See? If the dentist had his say-so,
he'd deal with the matter,
his way. When I was young, it was no trouble
skipping a brushing or two. When you're old, your body

remembers. Don't let anybody
kid you: *Que sera, sera* won't make you feel better
tomorrow. Tomorrow... Don't mind me. My old croak troubles
tin ears. Only time I sang was when my kids teethed.
Sure is nice to finally know what doesn't matter,
all those things my mother used to say—

same old things she heard her mother say:
"Take care of your children, your husband. You're nobody."
Women didn't matter
back then, we didn't need to better
our selves. Brush, sure. Floss, yes. But that was it, for teeth.
Sugar was the cause of a lot of our trouble,

a rotten way to keep us happy. Nothing but trouble
for a little indulgence. Now they say
be good to yourself, and your teeth:
don't put a teaspoon of sugar in your body.
Only eat what makes you feel better
on the inside. You're young, but maybe you know it matters—

not being a door mat.
Best thing for your health. You don't recognize trouble
until one day you know better—
we were driving his fixed-up car. Soon as I started to say:
"We need to turn around, I left something at the body shop,"
he leaned over, and socked me in the teeth.

I just want to say, it doesn't matter
when you have troubles—long as you have somebody
who helps you feel better when life knocks out your teeth.

Dear Impostor,

Do me a favor.
Bring back my husband.

I am leaden from living
with you, deadened from waiting
for my beloved to return
with eyes no longer vacant.

Tell me your ransom—
I'll pay it.

If all you seek is an antidote
to emptiness, I can help.
There's someone here
I want to present to you.

Impostor, meet mine.
Take her.

Warranty

My specialty is studying companies who care about their customers. Take Nordstrom's. They have a return policy that can't be beat. Once they refunded a customer her money for a tire she returned. They don't sell tires.

This Yom Kippur I would like you to be my Nordstrom's. I want to return to you slews of careening thoughts, wrecked words, sideswiping actions—even though you are not their rightful owner.

Hair

was the first thing
the Third Reich took.
It was already dead.

C-Word

It's not a flap of skin snipped
nor a covenant with god

It's not in the Torah
not in the Koran

It is a budding clitoris
        cut

two labia petals
        cut

It is three thorns and thread
        saving a small hole for urine
        the same small hole for semen

So there must be more cutting
        to release the first baby

cut again
        for the second

cut cut cut
        for the third, fourth, fifth

cutting of scar tissue
        too taut to stretch around a baby's head
        too taut to save a mother's life

And it all starts
        with nerve endings

it starts with a covenant
        of pain

starts with a five year-old girl
        her unsheathed screams

Tourist-attraction.com

Should you like what you see, do stop
surfing and linger. Kindly touch your

screen and we'll arrange your round-
trip ticket, so you may seek comfort in

the bodies you've been merely eyeing
on-line. Gentle sir, not to worry: we offer

the ultimate in discretion. And the girls
so enjoy your accent as much as your hard

currency. Never mind their bedroom eyes, sunken
like your imperial Roman baths. You'll soon spend

yourself in their small mouths, insatiably
open with hunger. So come, come

invest in Romania's future. Leave your marks
on this young democracy, prematurely

coming of age like a street-wise adolescent—
free to learn how to live hand to mouth.

My body

the consolation prize,
my holes the spoils of war,
my name is gynocide.

Congolese Calculus

When rape is

multiplied

by five

in a gang of men, raised

to incalculable power

in front of a husband

and children,

when rape

extends

to a stick, a torch, a bayonet, or a gun,

the genitals of

a woman

pried

open,

when the Congolese

army proved its mania

for 10 days

in Minova—looting, razing, raping

women

and girls—to lionize

victory in Goma, when out of

over 1,000,

nearly 75 victims

testified—their faces

veiled

to regain

their nullified lives—

and of the 39 accused—

25 rank

and file,

14 officers—

only two

junior soldiers were convicted—

one rape

apiece,

when just 30 cases

in 10 years of war

crimes and crimes

against

humanity have been tried

while the mass

of atrocities wreaked by

divisions of

armed forces are dismissed

as imaginary,

and when violence

traces

its roots

squarely

to colonial history when,

under Belgium's King

Leopold, women were equated

with bait—

and wives were cordoned

off from husbands

to increase production

rates—for the royal

harvest of rubber,

and if quotas were not

reached, hands

or arms were

severed—yet what still

remains

is not the sum

of parts,

but the integral

question: not where

did it begin,

but in which

fraction of humanity

will it end?

Confession

My daughter's latest letter said:
End this now, Daddy. No matter what

the shrinks say, I must be insane
to switch my pleas to guilty.

Twenty-two counts, count 'em!
They were asking for it.

The second one didn't even beg
till she saw the knife. The first—

just a cry baby. *Please! Please!*
Plea-eese! was all I heard.

I'm not the first—my father was
doing time before I was eight, before

I knew the difference between rape
and misconduct was minor.

But murder, that was easy for a kid
to figure out. I wonder about that girl—

if she tried to bargain with the old man,
or just plain pled to be spared.

He didn't have it in him to stop.
I know. He used to whip me till I'd buckle.

Between the snaps of leather, he'd yell:
I'm no man o' God, but I prayed—

Hell, I begged Him for a pretty little girl
and look what I got to put up with!

If he'd had a daughter instead of me,
I wouldn't be standing here handcuffed,

staring at my daughter's wrinkled-up
eighth-grade picture. Maybe we should line up—

the old man, the girl they never found,
my daughter, her two friends they found

in my backyard, and me. We could all
take a seat in the jury box, leave one empty

between each of us, and spend the rest of time
hearing how God pleads His case.

Enheduanna's Curse on Lugalanne

again and again
he throws a hateful verdict
in my face

        —Enheduanna, Sumerian High Priestess and
        the first known author of the world, 2285-2250 BCE

May the stars fool your pinprick eyes
with traitorous constellations of exile
May the moon god eclipse as you caravan
May the goddess snore through your pleas
You threw me out of the temple

May the scorched sands cushion your bed
May they sear your wanderlust body
May the bronze shimmer of heat erect
four blistering walls as your tent
I am not allowed in my rooms

May your cooking fire extinguish
beneath the wet rawness of game
May your wine skin leak trails for bandits
May your camels hawk when you yawn
You wiped your spit-soaked hand on my mouth

May your dagger be sharp as arrowheads
May your worm wriggle out of its sheath
May the blade you aimed at my sex
untether the dangling—

31

#TippiHedrenToo

Ravens swarm
with lust, swoop

down on the head
of the leery Hitch-

cock blonde.
Close-up: She stoops

to evade the spread
talons. Sir Alfred,

one gnawing query:
How many takes

for claws to grow
weary? How many cuts

to untangle two
stringy bird feet

from a teased
platinum bouffant?

Just pose this:
the pearly face

as it streaks black
from the unkindness

of ravens—or
your ravenous taunt.

In Brazil's Defense

In this kind of crime what is defended is not honor, but vanity,
and the pride of the lord who sees a woman as his personal property.
—Brazilian Supreme Court decision, 1991

Before. (In defense of honor)

                              Husbands   red-eyed

    lovers   killed

                              with impunity

    Lawyers won

                              acquittals   homicide

    legally

                              Women's bodies

    murdered

                              for cuckoldry

After. (In defense of economics)

                              Men   Brazil's wild heart-

    land

                              refused to abide

    Expensive

                              to divorce

33

cheaper

           save face   Hire

a gunslinger

           kill your wife

Widow's Choice

Roop Kanwar glowed in a billowing sari of flames—

                this newlywed widowed at 18, childless.

Did the 45 acquitted force her on the pyre?—

                    Or did she tempt the fire that left her lifeless?

Thousands watched this Rajput woman turn to ash and bone—

                the alchemy of *sati* rendered her chaste.

Pious flesh burned to arrest the remorseless cycle—

                better her husband's safe passage than disgrace.

Before the pyre, she apprehended a new sentence—

                  she could flee and embody austerity:

shave her head, eat boiled rice, sleep on coarse matting, face-down—

                    or on the river in a rippling sari.

Proverbs for Pashtun Women

Rahila Muska, 2010.

A false smile set my body on fire.
A man's hands pummeled my mouth shut for penning satire.

Malala Yousafzai, 2014.

Bullets fly in the face of freedom.
Books, not drones or bombs, stock my armory with reason.

Postcards from Croatia

The house is riddled with bullet holes.
The nursery window remains closed
as a child's mobile spins and slows.

Somewhere the canopy above the boles,
somewhere a couple's life unfolds.
The hours are riddled with bullet holes.

Somewhere soup brims in bowls.
Somewhere a toddler begins to doze
and a mobile spins as breathing slows.

Somewhere a field greens and rolls.
Somehow the birth of copper foals.
The horse is riddled with bullet holes.

Somewhere the cows loll and low—
some, where a barefoot girl outgrows
a child's mobile spinning slow.

Somewhere, a bell forgets to toll
and death forgets where to pose.
The hearse is riddled with bullet holes.
A child's mobile slows.

Legend of the Young Storyteller

Once there was a girl who wrote her stories
not in sun-dappled yellows and candy-apple reds,

but in the rising color
of bruised skin.

Not on the smooth pages
of crayon books, but on scrawled

walls of tissue and bone.
This girl told stories not in words that flew

like birds from her mouth—just a silence
that filled a fist.

One day the girl began to count her stories.
They were in her fingerprints.

She traced them in the sand—
story upon story—into a castle of words.

Then the tide swept in.
Her mouth opened like the "O"

of a conch and she trumpeted
a roiling ocean.

A Note Sor Juana Dreams of Sending to the Bishop of Puebla

So in my case, it is not seemly
that I be viewed as feminine,
as I will never be a woman
who may as woman serve a man.
— Sor Juana Inés de la Cruz, poet-nun of New Spain
and the first feminist of the Americas, 1648?-1695

First, I dream. Then I write
between the lines for fools
to abide by patriarchy's rules.
Make no mistake: I incite
The Most Reverend's tongue to spite.
Then, I recant, forswear:
No nun's desire will lay bare
in noble works of art.
Ban or burn my books. I take heart:
To confess your envy is my prayer.

II

To My Mother

How do I speak of my eyes, my hands?
To speak of them is to speak of you.

In each word I write
your name abides.

My hands are yours.
Not my feet, not my mouth.

I touch the swell of life—
my fingers brim.

And of my eyes?
I am color-blind—

only the prism of your laughter
on dark lakes.

Though while I sleep,
you trace rivers beneath my lids.

An Embarrassment of Euphemisms

White-scarfed mothers circling the Plaza de Mayo
Tie five words into a knot of truth—*(Uno: ¡Desaparecido!)*—

While the Dirty War turns protest to silence
And the rest is spun into speech absent
Of meaning—into terms of political correction—
As "prisoner assessment" equals "secret detention"
And numbers signify names
With attire reduced to hoods and chains

> *(Dos: ¡Torturado!)*

And the Nazi equivalent of "transfer" is resurrected as "death"
But first, "outings" suggest "beatings" and "near-drownings"
And "the grill" serves as "cremation" and after, the lashing
Río de la Plata becomes the tarnished river of ashes
Until "the flight" implies "the pit is brimming with flies"
And bodies—naked, drugged, alive—are dropped from the sky

> *(Tres: ¡Asesinado!)*

Then el Punto Final grants amnesty to the murder of crowing
Military as mothers encircle their arms into a mobbing wing.

> *(Never Forgotten! ¡Nunca Olvidado!)*

Eugenics Rant

A "feeble-minded" taxonomy

for females in the early twentieth century

spelled compulsory

sterility;

and for Native American women in the '60s,

"feeble" equaled unmarried pregnancy

or a white coat's verdict

of promiscuity;

and for 60% of black women in Sunflower County—

victims of "Mississippi appendectomies"—

and 1/3 of Puertorriqueñas in our pulsing territory

of bomba dances—due to their "hyper-fertility"

and their booming poverty—the US polity

decreed these ladies of the south

and commonwealth

failed to see their burden on society's health

and must tender their tubes

or wombs as the toll,

as the means to minority birth-control;

but if they were to rise to a higher station

and if they had a voice in this chosen nation,

they would certainly vote

for sterilization.

Kali Knocks on a Mother's Door

On the 4th of every month, Kali appears
as a child protective officer at the door
of an unsuspecting mother.

I wear a snarling mask to counter your lips curled
in shame. As I do your penance, your eyelids unfurl:

I roll my body in charcoal dust, then my ribs
imprint the earth with your child's sorrow.

For every act of silence and neglect,
I offer you a skull from my necklace.

No? You don't dare to draw near?
My viperous arms could uncoil your voice.

Or your hollow throat could remain closed—
swallow your lover's bladed words, his light touch

searing your child. You need my shadowy half
and cannot survive without the baring of teeth.

A Mother's Answer to Slavery
in Toni Morrison's Beloved Story

This is not a story to pass on. This is

a story that will eat you clean.

Start with your heart,

end with your feet. All four of them.

This is not a story to pass on. This

is a story that can break

your neck. From a rope on a tree,

from a handsaw near a mother's milk.

This is a story that can't set you free.

Free of ankle chains or neck rings

forged of red iron. This story

is a red ghost with 60 million faces,

a tree spreading its red branches

across a welted back, and a red

neck in the tender crook—

in a mother's arms—the blade

bleeding in her clenched fist.

I Did Not Name You El Negro

El Negro is our property.
—Carles Abella, Banyoles City Council, Spain

Your body was robbed by taxidermists
for wildlife displays in Paris.

Stuffed and preserved as El Negro,
you later stood at the Darder for show.

Your centuries in a vitrine,
your empty coffin beneath the sun.

From Banyoles to Botswana,
you are San, Bushman, Basarwa.

You were rendered unfit by critics
eyeing Barcelona's Olympics.

In 2000, your sacred remains—
only skull, bones—returned from Spain.

Beneath a Botswanan monument,
the quake of your exiled interment.

From Banyoles to Botswana,
you are San, Bushman, Basarwa.

I have waited since your first burial.
I have keened on the River Vaal.

I will not return to my grave—
you must rest where your story is saved.

They will not call you "the black one":
your name escapes from my tongue.

From Banyoles to South Africa,
you are my son, not Bushman, not Basarwa.

Your face

mirrors mine before you were sown—
child of Rwanda, child born of rape—
and on days I know you are mine alone.

A Linguist Stick Speaks Up

> *Although the hen knows it is dawn,*
> *she leaves it to the rooster to announce.*
> —Asante proverb, Ghana

My body is a long, lithe tongue
to plead, to barter: my skin
beaten golden into coils of snakes,
my finial an elephant poised
to trumpet. I stand in the hands
of the sturdy linguist—between
royalty and the rest who rely on his fluency
to represent their interests. But I am
merely a mouthpiece, a drum
for announcing and renouncing—
for the growl, the offering:
I am totem of wildcat and bushbuck.
I am *atoke, gankogui, axatse:*
bell, gong, beaded rattle of gourd.
I am the rooster that does not sleep.
And if I were to stick up for my matriline,
I would defer to the Golden Stool,
this seat of the Asante soul,
and conjure Yaa Asantewaa's return.
Let the Queen speak, not me, for valor:
If you, the men of Asante, will not go forward,
then we, the women, will. We will fight!—
for unity and the end to colonies.
Let her crowing usher in the dawn.

Blackbird's Revenge

A new 3m-high bronze cast of a… pearl diver… acknowledges the…
19th century practice of "blackbirding"—the forcible kidnapping of
Aboriginal women to… dive for pearls, often without breathing apparatus.
—Flip Prior, *The West Australian*, November 30, 2010

Once, her ebony body scavenged for breath

among cargos of ocean. Black gleamed

from irises— undersea magicians that enslaved the sun.

Now, dark wings kidnap the wind.

Unshackled talons return pearl

eggs to the womb of the sea.

And sky— her wild blue desert—

drowns out white: Dreamtime horizons.

Editorial on the Trinity: Mother, Sister, Bishop

Just days before Christmas, Bishop Thomas Olmsted stripped
St. Joseph's Hospital of its affiliation with the Roman Catholic diocese.
—Nicholas Kristof, *New York Times*, January 30, 2011

Margaret McBride has never been a bride:
no blushing cheek, attired in white or black.
A nun, the Church avows, must marry Christ,

obey His laws. This nun is under attack
for saving a woman facing certain death.
The bishop claims her sin is turning her back

on Mother Church and a fetus of waxing breadth
in a waning womb. Sister McBride approved
the abortion, put a woman above the rest.

A mother saved, a family spared. The proof?
Four small lives redeemed from grief.
For these good works, the Sister was reproved:

Bishop Olmstead proclaimed her choice, in brief,
worthy of excommunication. The Phoenix
hospital dared to hold a different belief.

Unheralded, the bishop issued the edict
to excommunicate the infidel—the hospital—
just days before the merry birth of Jesus.

In this season for misers, for the prodigal,
in this infirmary for the ill and the dying,
on Christmas there will ring no bells or gospel:

only the knelling of conscience, bonafide.

Mary Magdalene's Canticle

When thou tookest upon thee to deliver man,
Thou didst not abhor the Virgin's womb.
—from Te Deum, a prayer in the Liturgy of the Hours

Let us praise the exhumed wombs,
this closed pit of pelvic bones
from the silenced choir of corpses,
this Irish mass of the nameless.

Let us perfume their remains
from my alabaster jars:
anoint each skull with oil of myrrh,
bless each pelvis with rose hips.

From Matins to Compline, let us pray:
Hallowed be their resting place, this Glasnevin grave.

Let us chant for prostitutes—
rise up for fallen women—
join hands for unwed mothers,
claim and name their orphan children.

Let us magnify their sins:
beauty a treacherous siren,
virginity a starved beggar,
poverty a petty thief.

From Matins to Compline, let us pray:
Hallowed be the mound of this penitents' grave.

Let us forget the chafed hands,
lashes of leather by Mother,
razor-scraped scalps and shaved heads,
but not the private meetings with Father.

Let us forgive the convent—

Our Lady of Charity—
for profiting from Magdalene laundries,
for scouring the streets for slave labor.

From Matins to Compline, let us pray:
Hallowed be the laundresses in a whitewashed grave.

Let us build altars of barbed wire
and milk leaking from swollen breasts;
rip open adoption records:
fill arms emptied of infants.

Let us remember cremation,
then reburial by the Sisters,
the land developer who unearthed
remains in the first chaste grave.

From Matins to Compline, let us pray
for the 155 found in a Dublin convent grave.

Ballad of the Crone

Is Mary Magdalene a pope?
Apostle? Prostitute?
The Gnostic wife of Jesus Christ?
In Rome, the point is moot.

Old England's hags in fairy tales
left nightmares in their wake.
Now wizened spinsters' loveless trails
may favor lives of saints.

Once, Salem claimed the covens' curse
concocting spells and brews.
Soon, witch hunts rife with burning stakes—
so easy to accuse.

Teacher, healer, goddess, witch:
the woman is the same.
The only difference is the man—
his hoary choice of name.

Fortune Teller

The positions of Romani men and Romani women are clearly divided.
Unfortunately, women have drawn the losing card.
　　　　　—Sabina Xhemajli, Romani activist

Once I dressed as a gypsy: violet shawl
draped across my narrow shoulders and dirty-
blond mane, patchwork skirt scratching
my ankles, and dozens of jangling bracelets,

> *In the dark of the caravan you clench both hands*
> *into clanking fists. Your Romani palms refuse to be read.*

brassy on each wrist. I sat on a yellow metal
step stool pale as canary feathers, cold as the river
in winter, waiting for the young partygoer
to open the secret door in my parents' carport.
Under a single light bulb dangling from the rafters,
I consulted my black fortune ball—

> *Your hand flicks open: a long life line slashed—*
> *here, here, here—interrupted by bruised skin.*

no crystal—in the stuffy utility room crammed with washer,
dryer, water heater, lamp shades, rollerless luggage, my dad's
rock collection, my 21-speed bike, my sister's bike
with its cool banana seat, and me, a teenaged fortune teller
rented—like a snake charmer—to the neighbor across the street.

> *You retract your hand, coil both arms around your head,*
> *shaking your hair into a nest of black snakes.*

It was my piano teacher's daughter's tenth birthday
and I was the entertainment, rolling over
the eight ball resembling a pirate's eye patched
with black crepe blotting out the eight circled in white.

You hold up the candle to the purple ring
around your eye. Your coffee steams.

I read the fortune of each little girl-guest
and ignored the underside, the buoyant magic
words—"without a doubt" or "reply hazy…"—

Next, coffee grounds: you tread on hot coals.
You do not know when the fire will rage.

as I hid, in the billowy folds of my skirt,
the secret list with her name and favorite things.
After each saucer-eyed girl closed the door behind her,

You swallow the grounds—no, you spit them out,
lunging toward the half-door. Tarot calls you back.

I dried the sweat on my neck and forehead. How fortunate
I was to play dress-up as a teen, to work my dream job,
to pretend to see into someone else's future

Finally, the cards: bear, then sickle and skeleton.
Feed and keep the cubs in check. Or rear up on your hind legs.

when I could only dream about my own in the dark
broken by the light bulb swinging.

Message from the Black Madonna to the First Mothers

Some say I turned black from decay
of gold and azure pigments leaking lead.
Others credit centuries of grime,
of devotees' votive candle-smoke.

I say: Indigene, I belong to your kind.
I am Our Lady of Africa in Algiers,
Manila's Nuestra Señora de Guía,
La Guadalupana in Mexico City.

I am the brown, the black, of the earth.
I am the first to give birth, to nurse.
My skin is the primordial soil.
I open my dark palms to feed your kin.

I place one word on your Native tongue.
Say: *mawlud, napanganak, nacer.*
From Africa to Mexico, you are first-*born.*
Born beyond nations, born to the land.

Hand

the penultimate letter in *nacre*
to the word's end: for *nacer*
and the forgotten to be reborn.

Song for Nacre

O, lustrous iridescence
slick with pink, silver, violet.

You are the protector of flesh
lining abalone, coating oyster.

Your sticky sheath rains gems.
You glisten on the hilts of knives,

in dewdrop buttons, boxes
inlaid. Your beauty refutes age

while ours fades in fugitive images
of sepia, platinum, mercury and silver.

Milky mother-of-pearl, we rub
your sheen until our scaly skin gleams.

The Daughter I Sometimes Have

some dreams
hang in the air like smoke
touching everything.
                    —Lucille Clifton

1.

When I was seven, she appeared, old as earth, and just as solid. Each time I bit into my yellow No. 2 pencil, she pulled it from my mouth and placed it in my left hand. I didn't know it then, but she was the one making the stilted, gray marks. She pressed hard enough to leave traces of block letters five pages deep. I used to think she was a magician because she turned dull smudges into song. My teacher called her Graphite. But *she* told me she was born a black princess in Sri Lanka. Though she lived in the earth, I did not have to root for her. The hungry teeth came. Metal jaws cleaved her from home.

2.

Now she seems more like a dream, *like smoke hanging in the air touching everything.* She appears mostly at night: smoke more silver than my hair, smoke veiled by the dark. She feels more dangerous now, the way smoke can stop me from breathing. But she no longer presses hard against the page. The white coats press her to slow neutrons. They call her by her last name: Reactor. She only wants to spell uranium and slow *me* down—to ignite a chain reaction with bud and root, heart and lung, stone and wave. I want her to combust my scribbles into a radiant cloud that touches all things with rain.

Letter from Camille Claudel to Albert Einstein

Monsieur Einstein: I am told you are a genius,
that your new theories of relativity
will alter the face of science. But I think
you are more than a scientist since you see light
as an artist. I dare not discuss my thoughts
with anyone but you. Here in the asylum
the doctors and aides are as vacant as those like me
who have forsaken all trace of ourselves.
I sit surrounded by granite stares and marble eyes.
And when I turn I do not see a woman here,
a woman there. Only blocks of stone,
each waiting for its chisel to shape them
into something that resembles humanness.
And I am frightened by the beauty of it.
Perhaps you heard I was a sculptor, once.
My first love was stone—stroking its weight,
beguiling its light that refused to deny me.
You see, like you, I contemplated light.
Had you been more than a boy, we might have loved.
But I met Rodin. Amid the Gates of Hell,
we made love. And then I too was condemned:
Rodin was far less forgiving than stone.
If you were here, you might argue, dear Einstein,
that rock cannot be relative to Rodin.
But when two lovers are sculpted from one stone,
they are impossible to separate.
Some part of one, or both, will be lost—
a leg cleaved, an arm torn from embrace.
My brokenness returned me to my art.
Then as before, where others saw nothing,
I saw sparks: a woman kneeling near a hearth,
another imploring—her hand outstretched.
I began to capture smaller bundles of light.
Each one small enough to hold in your hand.
Critics deplored my work. I had no choice.
I had to make my art invisible—

the way the world already perceived it.
I began with the bust of beloved Rodin:
one day I picked up a hammer and struck each piece—
except for a handful of tiny figures.
Like the one I am mailing you, *mon ami*:
I call it *The Wave*. A few admired it once,
this wave in motion cupping three children.
When you cup it lightly in your palm,
I know you are the only one who will see
what is relative: this mass from my fingers,
your hand, and the energy cast between.

Dream Diary: Artist Sketch

Her paints pool in ice trays,

her easel jerry-rigged from old milk crates.

She wears overalls thick with grime, denim sleeves

rolled high, second-hand boots laced tight.

In a tool shed with small, south-facing windows,

she begins. First, a gray undercoat

she has ground from chewed pencils.

Next, she applies mud

and straw. The ghost of a devil-

fork dead-center.

She never sits. Tall,

all backbone, with stumps for legs.

She spreads paint with her knuckles,

thickens pigment with calloused fingers.

No brushes. But knives

for scraping. She paints the way she lives.

There can be too much light,

too much temptation to set down her grit. Mud

splatter and straw and scraped

grays. She pulls down the shade, halfway.

Outside, the mockingbird calls and calls.

She doesn't hear.

She is sawing wood to gird canvases.

No frames for her paintings:

Their stories survive on their own.

.

In the Cypress and Cedar Box

Five white scarves knotted into an egret's wing.

One hand mirror and one fired bullet.

A vitrine with a skull. A coffer of rubber rings (guarded by a snarling mask).

Consolation prizes: a leaky wine skin, two stringy bird feet, and a one-way ticket on an unknown airline.

Hand-written birth certificates (with rebirth dates in gold and azure pigments).

Studies in gray (and a chewed No. 2 pencil). One stone sculpture of a wave small enough to hold in your palm.

8th grade pictures, unwrinkled. A flesh-tone door mat, unstained.

Indigo pillows embroidered with honorable court decisions. (Transcripts of dishonorable ones have been burned.)

Saris the color of flames. And a talisman of smoke.

An alabaster jar of myrrh and rose hips.

A red branch. Dried willow leaves.

Sprinkle a handful of ash. Leave box open in sunlight and rain. Wait for volunteers to grow.

Willow

The willow's green cauldron calls to me.
It's 40 years since I climbed the old ash,
my childhood sentinel. Last time I saw
its canopy reach for the curb, new plumes
of sky sifted through the heavy branches.
I sat across the street in a red rental
pardoning the four cars in the driveway
for their unfamiliar, colorless bodies.
Two hours before, my mother died
at 3:24—the same smudged number
on the wooden mailbox with the flag down.
This was the last day I would see
all my safe places. I didn't dare
knock on the front door or toll the bell
next to the back door in the carport.
But if I had, I'd have clanged twice and then run
to climb the ash to unbury my sorrow—
to imagine poems or gaze through this pane-
less window into neighbor's lives. Nothing
stirred but the bird flapping in my chest.
Here, in my meadow 2,000 miles northwest,
the willow drapes at my feet. I reach up, climb in.

Dream Diary: Invocation

The moon's   unblinking   eye   slices   the dark.

     A windless   night   and   the aspens   stand   mute.

     In this circle   of trees,   I throw up my hands,

rending the thick   air.   Rising   and bowing,

     again   and again,   my splayed   fingers

     claw   the emptiness   pregnant

     with   everything   lost:

with   the bound   feet   of unwanted   girls,

     the kidnapping   of school   girls,

     trafficking   of child-   girls,

     torture   of activist   girls,

     beating   of wife-   girls,

the molesting

     of small-

     boned   girls.

     ~ ~ ~

A low,   gurgling   croak: she   is here.

     I want to   quiet   the shrill.

But   there are   too many   predators,

too many   nests   disturbed.

I scan   the trees   for wings

to shroud   darkness,   render it   invisible.

I can   only   rasp,   *Raven*   *Woman,*

call   *to me*   *with light.*

The darkness   lurches:

she tips one wing   at the sky,

the other   at the grove—   these   aspens

now   a radiant   silver   beneath   the new moon.

And her   gurgling   turns   to grating:

Stand tall   *among*   *the Upright*   *People.*

The air quakes   as her   wings   breathe

the trees   like lungs.   In her   wake,

a murmuring: *Stir*

like aspen.

Make   *a rush*   *of sound*

that shakes   *the world.*

Notes

Epigraph—These are the opening lines of "Woman in the Painting" from *Landscape with Female Figure: New and Selected Poems, 1982-2012* by Andrea Hollander.

"Arranged Marriage"—"Ardent spirits" refer to strong, alcoholic liquors made by distillation. Until the passing of the Married Women's Property Act in 1870, a wife had no independent existence under English law and, therefore, no right to own property or to enter into contracts separately from her husband, or to sue for divorce or for the control and custody of her children.

"Columbia Gorge Dance Card"—"Milonga campera" is a type of Argentine tango. Tango flourished on the back streets of brothels and bordellos in Buenos Aires during the large-scale wave of immigration (of mostly men) in the 1880s. The "bandoñeón," a type of concertina introduced from Germany in 1880, is the essential instrument in Argentine tango.

"C-Word"—This poem was inspired by the documentary *Half the Sky* (2012) based on the book *Half the Sky: Turning Oppression into Opportunity for Women Worldwide* (2008) by Nicholas D. Kristof and Sheryl WuDunn.

"Tourist-attraction.com"—Andrea Bruce's article "Romania's Disappearing Girls: Poverty, desperation drive girls from their hometowns & into the arms of sex traffickers" published in Aljeezera America on August 9, 2015 indicates: "According to the U.S. State Department's 2014 'Trafficking in Persons' report, one-third of Romania's trafficking victims are underage girls... The Eurostat 2015 report notes that Romania was one of the top five countries of origin for victims of human trafficking in the EU." [http://projects.aljazeera.com/2015/08/sex-trafficking-in-romania/index.html]

"Congolese Calculus"—According to the 2016 article "The actual state of sexualized violence in the Democratic Republic of Congo" by Laura Wolfe, Director of Women Under Siege at the Women's Media Center in New York, "DRC ranked 149th out of 188 countries on the 2014 Gender Inequality Index, a measurement compiled by the UN Development Program." In Wolfe's 2012 article "Shocking attitudes point to deep misogyny in Congo," she quotes Dr. Denis Mukwege, 2018 Nobel Peace Prize laureate and founder of Congo's Panzi Hospital which supports survivors of sexual assault: "When you talk about rape in New York or Paris, everyone can always say, 'Yes, we have rape here too.' But it's not the same thing when a woman is raped by four or five people at the same time, when a woman is raped in front of her husband and children, when a woman is not just raped but then after the rape her genitals are attacked with a gun, a stick, a torch, or a bayonet. That's not what you see in New York. That's not what you see in Paris." [http://www.womenundersiegeproject.org/] Details on the Minova rape case can be found on the Human Rights Watch Website: https://www.hrw.org/report/2015/10/01/justice-trial/lessons-minova-rape-case-democratic-republic-congo. An exploration of DRC's colonial atrocities can be found in *King Leopold's Ghost: A Story of Greed, Terror, and Heroism in Colonial Africa* by Adam Hothschild.

"Confession"—This poem is informed by news reporting on Ward Francis Weaver III, a convicted felon serving a life sentence without parole for sexual assault, rape, attempted murder, and the 2002 murders of Ashley Pond and Miranda Gaddis in Oregon City, Oregon.

"Enheduanna's Curse on Lugalanne"—Enheduanna (2285-2250 BCE) was a Sumerian High Priestess and the first known author of the world. The epigraph and italicized lines are excerpted from "Nin-Ma-Šár-Ra," a hymn to the goddess Inanna in which Enheduanna chronicles the tale of being thrown out of the temple by Lugalanne. The ruler of the city of Uruk, Lugalanne attempted to wrest power from Enheduanna's father, King Sargon of the Akkadian Empire.

"#TippiHedrenToo"—The October 30, 2016 *Variety* article, "Tippi Hedren Claims Alfred Hitchcock Sexually Assaulted Her in the '60s," by Alex Stedman details Tippi Hedren's claims of sexual assault and harassment by Alfred Hitchcock. Her memoir *Tippi* (William Morrow, 2016) and the movie "The Girl" (based on Donald Spoto's 2009 book, *Spellbound by Beauty: Alfred Hitchcock and His Leading Ladies*) further explore these claims.

"In Brazil's Defense"—According to James Brooke's article, "Honor Killing is Outlawed in Brazil" published in the *New York Times* on March 29, 1991, "Brazil's Supreme Court has ruled that a man can no longer kill his wife and win acquittal on the ground of 'legitimate defense of honor'... The 'defense of honor' strategy has been used by lawyers to win acquittals in thousands of cases of men on trial for murdering their wives. According to a study in São Paulo State for the period 1980-81, 722 men claimed defense of their honor as justification for killing women accused of adultery."

"Widow's Choice"—"Sati" (also spelled "suttee") is an obsolete Hindu funerary custom where a widow immolates herself on her husband's pyre or commits suicide in another fashion shortly after her husband's death. Initially legalized by the British, the practice (estimated at 500–600 instances of *sati* per year) was outlawed in 1829 in their territories in India, followed by a general ban for the whole of India issued by Queen Victoria in 1861. Following the outcry after the *sati* of Roop Kanwar on September 4, 1987, the Indian Government enacted the Rajasthan Sati Prevention Ordinance, 1987 and later passed the Commission of Sati (Prevention) Act, 1987. Some reports claim that Roop Kanwar was forced to her death by attendees who were present while contradictory reports claim that she told her brother-in-law to light the pyre when she was ready. Though inquiries resulted in 45 people being charged with her murder, they were acquitted. In addition, 11 people, including state politicians, were charged with glorification of *sati,* all of whom were also acquitted. From 1943-1987, there were 30 cases of *sati* or attempted *sati* in India. A "doha" is a Hindi form of poetry consisting of a rhymed couplet with 24 syllables in each line: 13 syllables followed by a caesura and then the remaining 11 syllables.

"Proverbs for Pashtun Women"—Rahila Muska is a pseudonym used by an Afghan teenaged girl ("muska" means "smile" in Pashto) to write poetry forbidden to women in Afghanistan. After being severely beaten by her brothers upon discovering her writing, she burned herself in protest and subsequently died. Malala Yousafzai is the youngest-ever Nobel Peace Prize laureate. She is a human rights activist for education and for women in her native Swat Valley in the Khyber Pakhtunkhwa province of northwest Pakistan, where the local Taliban had banned girls from attending school. Yousafzai survived a bullet to the forehead when she was shot by a Taliban gunman on her school bus on the afternoon of October 9, 2012. A "landay" is a Pashtun folk couplet with 22 syllables: nine in the first line, thirteen in the second. According to poet and journalist Eliza Griswold, "Traditionally, landays are sung aloud, often to the beat of a hand drum, which, along with other kinds of music, was banned by the Taliban from 1996 to 2001, and in some places, still is." [https://www.poetryfoundation.org/media/landays.html]

"Postcards from Croatia"—This poem was created in response to the photograph "Lost Innocence" taken by Russell J. Young in Croatia in 2004. [www.russelljyoung.com]

"A Note Sor Juana Dreams of Sending to the Bishop of Puebla"—The poem's epigraph is from "In Reply to a Gentleman from Peru, Who Sent Her Clay Vessels While Suggesting She Would Better Be a Man," in *Sor Juana Inés de la Cruz: Poems, Protest, and a Dream*, translated by Margaret Sayers Peden (Penguin, 1997). Sor Juana (1648?-1695) was a seventeenth-century poet-nun in colonial Mexico who wrote the first published feminist manifesto of the Americas, *Respuesta a sor Filotea de la Cruz (Reply to Sister Filotea of the Cross)*, in response to the Bishop of Puebla. Her advocacy for the education and erudition of women is also evident in her poem "Primero Sueño" ("First I Dream"). After mounting pressure from the Bishop of Puebla and her Confessor, Sor Juana abjured, giving away most of her work, along with her significant collections of books and musical and astronomical instruments. She died soon after, tending the sick. A "décima" is a Spanish Baroque form of poetry comprised of 10 octosyllabic lines with the rhyme scheme: abbaaccddc.

"An Embarrassment of Euphemisms"—The Dirty War in Argentina was waged from 1976 to 1983 by the military dictatorship against suspected leftist opposition. Estimates of those "disappeared" and killed range from 10,000 to 30,000. Translations of the Spanish follow:

- uno, dos, tres: one, two, three;
- desaparecido: the "disappeared" one;
- torturado: the tortured one;
- Río de la Plata: literally, "the River of Silver";
- asesinado: the assassinated one;
- el Punto Final: literally, "the final point"; the law passed in Argentina in 1986 which ended prosecutions for crimes perpetrated by the dictatorship;
- nunca olvidado: never forgotten.

Mobbing in animals is an anti-predator behavior which occurs when individuals of a certain species mob a predator by cooperatively attacking or harassing it, usually to protect their offspring. This is most frequently seen in avian species.

"Eugenics Rant"—In 1930, thirty U.S. states had laws advocating for the sterilization of the criminal, the mentally-ill, and the mentally-retarded. Many women were sent to institutions under the guise of being "feeble-minded" because they were promiscuous or became pregnant while unmarried. Activist Angela Davis in *Women, Race, and Class* (1981) states that women of predominantly ethnic minorities (such as Native American and African-American women) were sterilized against their will in many states, often without their knowledge while they were in a hospital for other reasons (e.g., childbirth). Sara Kugler's 2014 article on msnbc.com, "Day 17: Mississippi appendectomies and reproductive justice," confirms: "In 1967, the government admitted sterilizing 3,406 American Indian women without their permission." [http://www.msnbc.com/msnbc/day-17-mississippi-appendectomies] A "Mississippi appendectomy" was an unwanted, unrequested and unwarranted hysterectomy given to poor and unsuspecting Black women. According to pbs.org, Fannie Lou Hamer, co-founder of the Mississippi Freedom Democratic Party in the 1960s, told a Washington, D.C. audience in 1964 (three years after her own "Mississippi appendectomy") that "[in] the North Sunflower County Hospital… about six out of ten Negro women that go to the hospital are sterilized." [https://www.pbs.org/wgbh/americanexperience/features/freedomsummer-hamer/] From the beginning of the 1900s, U.S. and Puerto Rican governments espoused rhetoric connecting the poverty of Puerto Rico with overpopulation and the "hyper-fertility" of Puerto Ricans. Such rhetoric combined with eugenics ideology of reducing "population growth among a particular class or ethnic group because they are considered…a social burden" was the philosophical basis for the 1937 birth control legislation enacted in Puerto Rico. As of 1977, Puerto Rico had the highest proportion of childbearing-aged persons sterilized in the world. "Bomba" is a musical expression created in the late 17th century by West Africans who worked the colonial sugar plantations along the coast of Puerto Rico. At "bailes de bombas" (bomba dances), the fiery rhythms of drums called "barriles," originally made of empty codfish or rum barrels, draw the crowd into a circle. Dancers take turns challenging the drums, creating a dialogue with their movements that the solo drummer answers. It is said that women bomba dancers once danced with their skirts raised, showing their slips, to ridicule the attire worn by plantation ladies.

"Kali Knocks on a Mother's Door"—This poem was inspired by Caryl Campbell's artwork "Meeting Kali." [www.carylcampbell.com] In Hinduism, Kali is the fearful and ferocious form of the mother goddess. She is depicted as a multiple-armed figure wearing a garland of skulls.

"A Mother's Answer to Slavery in Toni Morrison's Beloved Story"—This poem is inspired by Toni Morrison's novel *Beloved*. "This is not a story to pass on" appears multiple times near the end of the book.

"I Did Not Name You El Negro"—"El Negro of Banyoles" is the name given to a stuffed human body that was displayed at the Francesc Darder Museum of Natural History in Banyoles, Spain between 1916 and 1997. It was removed after protests by Africans and people of African ancestry, which began around the time of the 1992 Barcelona Olympics. The body was repatriated to Africa and re-buried in Gaborone, capital of Botswana, on October 5, 2000. According to the article "Stuffed man going to 'wrong' home" by Rachel Rawlins published on September 28, 2000 in BBC News Online, "His body had been stolen by the Verraux brothers, two famous French taxidermists, the night after his burial some time in 1830. The location of the theft was narrowed down to the area around an old abandoned village called Kgatlane on the Vaal near the Orange River in South Africa." [http://news.bbc.co.uk/2/hi/africa/943616.stm] The people known commonly as the Bushmen are members of various Khoisan-speaking indigenous hunter-gatherer people representing the first nations of Southern Africa, whose territories span Botswana, Namibia, Angola, Zambia, Zimbabwe, Lesotho and South Africa. Though they call themselves by the names of their individual nations, they have been collectively referred to by others as San, Bushmen, and Basarwa. Each of these terms has a problematic history. According to the editorial "San, Bushman, or Basarwa: What's in a Name?" published in *Mail & Guardian* on September 5, 2007, Stephen Corry, indigenous rights activist and Director of Survival International, claims: "'San' has similarly pejorative roots, as does 'Basarwa.'" The same editorial cites a 1902 Dutch dictionary (in translation): "The word ['*bosch(jes)man*'] meant 'one who lives in the bushes' but had also been applied to apes, particularly the orangutan." Noves rimades ("rhymed news") is a French form of poetry consisting of octosyllabic rhymed couplets which was used by Catalan poets beginning in the fourteenth century.

"Your face"—This poem is inspired by Jonathan Torgovnik's photography exhibit "Intended Consequences: Children Born of Rape." [http://www.blueskygallery.org/exhibition/jonathan-torgovnik/#1]

"A Linguist Stick Speaks Up"—This poem was created in response to an Akan linguist staff at the Museum of Fine Arts in Houston. The Asante, or Ashanti, people live in southern Ghana and are the largest sub-grouping of the Akan people. "Atoke, gankogui, axatse" are "bell, gong, beaded gourd rattle," respectively. Yaa Asentewaa (circa 1840–1921) was appointed queen mother of Ejisu in the Ashanti Empire by her brother Nana Akwasi Afrane Okpese, the ruler of Ejisu. In 1900, she led the Ashanti rebellion known as the War of the Golden Stool against British colonialism. Yaa Asentewaa's full speech and details on the War of the Golden Stool can be found in Molefi Kete Asante's *History of Africa: The Quest for Eternal Harmony*.

"Blackbird's Revenge"—According to Flip Prior's article, "Tribute to Broome's Forgotten Women," in *The West Australian* on November 30, 2010: "A new 3m-high bronze cast of a female Aboriginal pearl diver… appears graceful at first glance. But a closer look reveals… the woman is pregnant and… gasping for air." In this article, Djugan and Yawuru woman Mary Theresa Torres Barker retells stories from her grandmother Polly Drummond about the "sad time" in Broome's history: "They found the women had the lung capacity to stay underwater longer—they were the best. Sometimes they used to go a little bit further and they would put the women in respirators but tie stones to their legs to keep them down." In Australian Aboriginal mythology, "Dream-time" means "eternal" or "uncreated."

"Editorial on the Trinity: Mother, Sister, Bishop"—This poem was inspired by Nicholas Kristof's article in the *New York Times* on January 30, 2011.

"Mary Magdalene's Canticle"— This poem was inspired by Steve Humphries' documentary *Sex in a Cold Climate* (1998). [https://www.youtube.com/watch?v=FtxOePGgXPs] The Magdalene Laundries, also known as Magdalene asylums, were Roman Catholic institutions that operated in Ireland from the 18th to the late 20th centuries. An estimated 30,000 women were confined in these Irish institutions. In 1993, a mass grave containing 155 corpses was uncovered in the convent grounds of one of the Dublin laundries run by Our Sisters of the Lady of Charity. This led to media revelations about the operations of the secretive institutions. A formal state apology was issued in 2013 and a compensation scheme for survivors was set up, to which the Catholic Church refused to contribute. According to Niall O Sullivan's article "Magdalene compensation snub is 'rejection of Laundry women'" in the August 2, 2013 issue of the *The Irish Post,* "It has emerged that all four of the religious congregations that ran the brutal Laundries have rejected personal appeals from Ireland's Justice Minister to make a financial contribution to the Irish Government's £50m [million] redress scheme." By the end of the 5th century, the Liturgy of the Hours—the official set of prayers marking the hours of each day— was composed of seven offices beginning with Matins (during the night, often at midnight) and ending with Compline (before retiring, generally at 9 pm). The Church obliges recitation of these prayers by nuns and monks.

"Fortune Teller"—According to Romani activist Sabina Xhemajli in a roundtable discussion of Romani women's rights on April 12, 2000, "The task of the Romani woman is to take care of the children, to maintain the household, and to hold together the extended family. As mother, she knows precisely the details of her children's lives, including all of the stupid things they do. She often hides this knowledge from her husband because she knows that she can expect harsh punishment for herself and her children." [http://www.errc.org/article/romani-women-in-romani-and-majority-societies/626]

"Message from the Black Madonna to the First Mothers"—A Black Madonna is a statue or painting of the Blessed Virgin Mary in which she is depicted with dark skin. *Nuestra Señora de Guía* means Our Lady of Guidance. *La Guadalupana* is another name for Mexico's *Virgen de Guadalupe,* or Our Lady of Guadalupe. *Mawlud, napanganak,* and *nacer* mean "born" in Arabic, Tagalog, and Spanish, respectively.

"Hand"—"Nacer" is the Spanish infinitive "to be born."

"The Daughter I Sometimes Have"—Graphite is used as a moderator in nuclear reactors to slow down neutrons to interact with Uranium-235 nuclei to continue the chain reaction.

"Letter from Camille Claudel to Albert Einstein"—Camille Claudel (1864–1943) was a French sculptor who became Rodin's apprentice, muse, and lover. She was the elder sister of the poet and diplomat Paul Claudel who, on March 10, 1913, committed her to the psychiatric hospital of Ville-Évrard in Neuilly-sur-Marne. Prior to this, she destroyed most of her work. Once in the asylum, she never created again. Her remaining sculptures are on display in the Musée Rodin.

"Dream Diary: Artist Sketch"—The original version of this poem was created in response to Edward Mitchell Bannister's "Seaweed Gatherers" (1898).

"Dream Diary: Invocation"—Ravens make short, repeated, shrill calls when chasing predators or trespassers, and deep, rasping calls when their nests are disturbed. In Haida mythology, the Raven is a trickster who steals light (i.e., the sun, moon, and stars) to give to mankind.

Source Acknowledgments

Grateful acknowledgment is made to the literary publications and theatrical performances in which these poems first appeared:

Amazing Eclectic Anthology (editor: John Garmon): "For Remembering"; "A Note Sor Juana Dreams of Sending to the Bishop of Puebla"; "Kali Knocks on a Mother's Door"; "Dream Diary: Artist Sketch"; "Dream Diary: Invocation"

Artlines2: Art Becomes Poetry: "A Linguist Stick Speaks Up"

Crab Orchard Review: "Tourist-Attraction.com"

Echoes Cabaret (producer: Jewish Theatre Collective): "An Embarrassment of Euphemisms"

Levure Litteraire: "What She Said When I Smiled at Her across the Table"; "Postcards from Croatia"

Lilith: "To My Mother" (forthcoming)

WA 129+ (editor: Tod Marshall): "Willow"

"A Linguist Stick Speaks Up" was a finalist in the 2015 Artlines2 ekphrastic poetry competition judged by Robert Pinsky and sponsored by Public Poetry and the Museum of Fine Arts in Houston.

"An Embarrassment of Euphemisms" was performed by the Jewish Theatre Collective as part of *Echoes Cabaret* at Milagro Theatre in Portland, Oregon on January 25-27, 2015.

About the Author

Poet-dramatist **Cindy Williams Gutiérrez** is inspired by the silent and silenced voices of history and herstory. Her latest collection, *Inlay with Nacre*, was awarded the Willow Books' 2018 Editor's Choice Selection and the 2016 Oregon Literary Fellowship for Writers of Color. A recipient of the 2017 Oregon Book Award for Drama, her play *Words That Burn* premiered at Milagro Theatre in Portland, Oregon in 2014. Cindy was selected by *Poets & Writers Magazine* as a 2014 Notable Debut Poet for her collection, *the small claim of bones* (Bilingual Press), which placed second in the 2015 International Latino Book Awards. Cindy earned an MFA from the University of Southern Maine Stonecoast Program with concentrations in Mesoamerican poetics, drama, and creative collaboration. Her website is **www.grito-poetry.com**.

More Praise for *Inlay with Nacre*

In an era of "Me Too," this collection is necessary reading. Gutiérrez remembers the stories of forgotten women and girls from different countries who have been abused, assaulted, kidnapped, raped, and murdered. While the poet witnesses the "unsheathed screams" of gynocide, she also "unfurls fists of silence" into a "rush of sound that shakes the world." These poems—like the people they honor—are pearls: strong, resilient, and iridescent.
—CRAIG SANTOS PEREZ, author of *from unincorporated territory*

With an impressive global reach, Gutiérrez builds a collection about the diminishment, abuse, resilience and resurgence of women. In the powerful penultimate poem, she returns home for her mother's funeral: "Nothing/ stirred but the bird flapping in my chest." And so the poems stir, an incantation from daughter to mother, woman to woman, fierce poems for our feminist times.
—FRANCES PAYNE ADLER, Professor Emerita and Founder,
   Creative Writing and Social Action Writing Program,
   California State University Monterey Bay

Bearing witness to resistance as well as brutality, *Inlay with Nacre: The Names of Forgotten Women* unearths the harrowing continuity of gender oppression globally and historically. In forceful narrative poems of exquisite clarity, Gutiérrez connects the stories of a Sumerian High Priestess, a poet-nun of colonial Mexico, female Aboriginal pearl divers and so many more women, beautifully fulfilling the title's sacred promise.
—DR. JESSICA MAUCIONE, Professor of English and
   Women's and Gender Studies, Gonzaga University

Poetry becomes activism in *Inlay with Nacre: The Names of Forgotten Women*. Gutiérrez's beautifully crafted poems compel the reader to feel the injustice of marginalized women. Individually, the poems are powerful and evocative. As a collection, they are a tour de force.
—DR. ELIZABETH URSIC, Women's Caucus Co-chair at the
   American Academy of Religion and author of *Women, Ritual, and Power*

CPSIA information can be obtained
at www.ICGtesting.com
Printed in the USA
FSHW011635100919
61889FS